In the Heart of the Forest

Written by Dave Murphy
Illustrated by Jennifer Davidson

Published by Bow River Books, an imprint of Deep Stance Media
Calgary, Alberta, Canada
www.bowriverbooks.com

Print Book ISBN 978-1-998568-08-6
E-Book ISBN 978-1-998568-09-3

This book is dedicated to all those
who lost their silent battles, and
to those still fighting.

You are not alone.

Once upon a time, in a cozy forest glade surrounded by tall trees and fluttering butterflies, there lived a fox named Felix.

Felix was not like the other foxes. He was smaller and quieter, with fur the color of autumn leaves. But what set Felix apart the most was his sadness.

Ever since Felix was a kit, whenever he saw coyotes, he would get scared.

He remembered a time when the forest was not peaceful. He was once out for a stroll in the woods when two coyotes chased him, but he managed to escape.

Sometimes he would think about the coyotes, and he often woke up shaking and afraid.

The other animals didn't understand why Felix was always so jumpy, and sometimes they teased him.

One sunny morning, Felix was hiding in a bush when he heard a soft voice say, "Hello, there." Felix peeked out and saw a wise old owl perched on a branch above him. The owl's feathers were a mixture of grays and whites, and his eyes twinkled with kindness.

"Why are you hiding, young Felix?" the owl asked gently.

Felix shuffled his paws nervously. "I-I'm scared of coyotes. They remind me of a time when the forest was scary."

The owl nodded wisely. "Ah, I see. You have a brave heart, Felix. It's not easy to carry those memories. But let me tell you something important: being brave doesn't mean you're never afraid. It means facing your fears, little by little."

Felix wasn't sure he understood, but he listened intently as the owl continued. "Every day, the forest wakes up to the sunrise, and every night it sleeps under the stars. Just like the forest, you can learn to find peace again. You can be brave."
Felix thought about what the owl said. Could he really be brave like the owl suggested?

That evening, as the sun dipped below the horizon and painted the sky in hues of pink and orange, Felix took a deep breath. He ventured out of his hiding spot and sat under the stars, watching as they twinkled above him.

"I want to be brave," Felix whispered to himself. "I want to find peace."
Days turned into weeks, and with each sunrise and sunset, Felix practiced being brave. He faced his fear of coyote sounds by listening to the gentle rustling of the leaves and the soothing song of the river.

He made friends with a family of rabbits who taught him how to hop and play without worry.

One day, as Felix was exploring a new part of the forest, he heard a coyote howl. His heart pounded, but instead of hiding, he remembered the owl's words. He took a deep breath and counted to three. "One, two, three," Felix whispered. "I am brave."

Felix felt a sharp pain in his leg and when he looked down, he saw his foot stuck in a fox trap. He yelled for help and a coyote appeared out of a nearby bush. "Looks like you need some help," the coyote said.

Felix said to the coyote, "You aren't going to hurt me?"

The coyote said, "Just because the past taps you on the shoulder, it doesn't mean you have to turn around and look." The coyote then freed him from the trap and walked away.
From that day on, Felix felt stronger and happier. He still remembered the scary times, but now he knew how to find his brave heart whenever he needed it.

And so, in the heart of the forest where the trees whispered secrets and the birds sang melodies, Felix the fox learned that even in the darkest of times, there is always hope and courage waiting to be found.

I wrote this book based on my personal struggles with PTSD for over 25 years. I was involved in a violent incident that deeply affected me and as a dad of a 10-year-old daughter I never knew how to talk to her about it or what I was going through.

My hope is to get this book in the hands of anyone who has battled trauma or is fighting silent battles, and for them to know that it's okay to ask for help. For me, it was the best thing I ever did.

If you would like to know more about my story, please scan the QR code to the right.

Thank you, and NEVER QUIT!
–*Dave Murphy*

Jennifer Davidson is an illustrator in Alberta, Canada. You can scan this QR code to learn more about her work:

Also from Dave Murphy

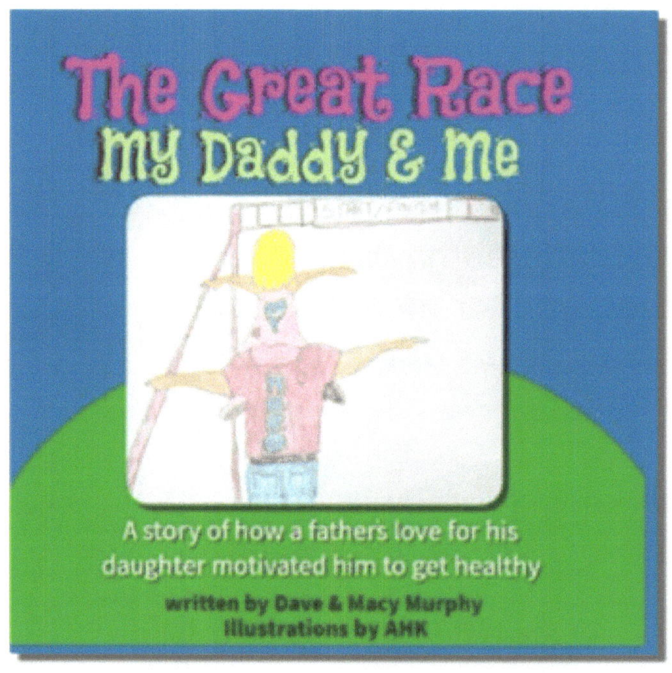

Also from Bow River Books

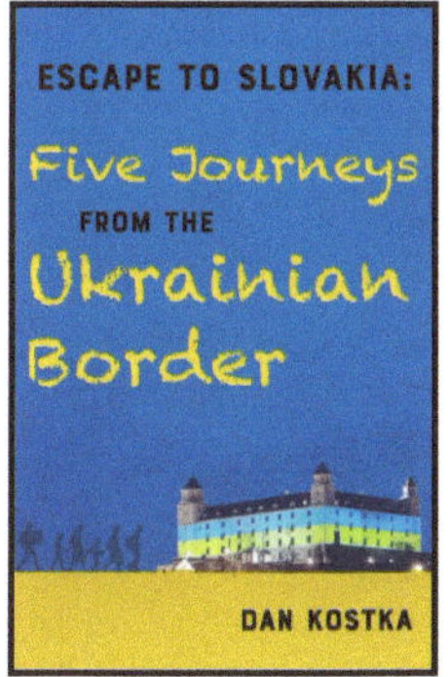

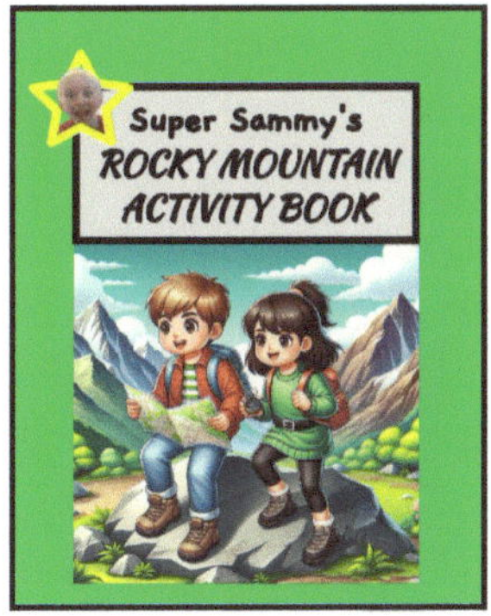

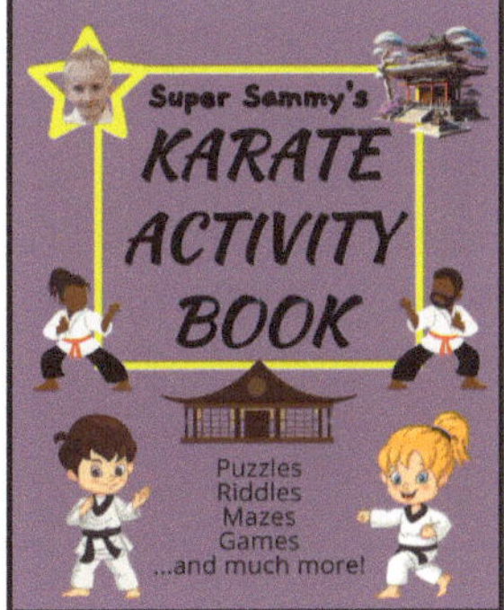

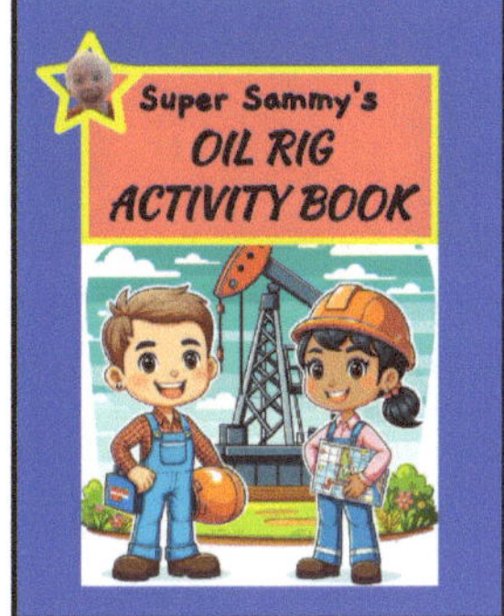

www.bowriverbooks.com